W9-AHQ-359

Presidents

JIMMY CARTER

A MyReportLinks.com Book

Tim O'Shei

MyReportLinks.com Books

an imprint of

 Enslow Publishers, Inc. E

Box 398, 40 Industrial Road
Berkeley Heights, NJ 07922
USA

To C. D. and L. M.,
thanks for your presidential help!

MyReportLinks.com Books, an imprint of Enslow Publishers, Inc.

Copyright © 2002 by Enslow Publishers, Inc.

Library of Congress Cataloging-in-Publication Data

O'Shei, Tim.
  Jimmy Carter : a MyReportLinks.com book / Tim O'Shei.
      p. cm. — (Presidents)
Includes bibliographical references and index.
Summary: Explores the career and influences of the president who worked
to preserve wildlife and national parks and to establish peace among
conflicting nations. Includes Internet links to Web sites, source
documents, and photographs related to Jimmy Carter.
  ISBN 0-7660-5051-3
  1. Carter, Jimmy, 1924– —Juvenile literature. 2. Presidents—United
States—Biography—Juvenile literature. 3. Human rights workers—United
States—Biography—Juvenile literature. [1. Carter, Jimmy, 1924– 2.
Presidents.] I. Title. II. Series.
  E873 .O84 2002
  973.926'092

                                 2001006224

Printed in the United States of America

10 9 8 7 6 5 4 3 2 1

Photo Credits: © Corel Corporation, pp. 1 (background), 3; Courtesy of
Academy of Achievement: Hall of Public Service, p. 25; Courtesy of America
Votes, p. 29; Courtesy of Habitat for Humanity, p. 43; Courtesy of Jimmy Carter
N.H.S. Education Program, pp. 14, 24; Courtesy of MyReportLinks.com Books,
p. 4; Courtesy of Plains, Georgia: Home of the 39th President of the United
States, pp. 16, 18, 19; Courtesy of The Carter Center, p. 41; Jimmy Carter
Library, pp. 1, 17, 21, 22, 30, 31, 35, 36; *The Charlotte Observer*, p. 33.

Cover Photos: © Corel Corporation; Jimmy Carter Library.

Contents

Report Links. 4

Highlights 10

1 The Fight For Peace, 1978 11

2 Growing Up, 1924–1942. 15

3 Rising to the Presidency,
   1943–1972 21

4 Election to the White House,
   1973–1976 27

5 Issues in Office, 1976–1980. 32

6 After the Presidency 39

   Chapter Notes. 45

   Further Reading 47

   Index 48

MyReportLinks.com Books
Great Books, Great Links, Great for Research!

MyReportLinks.com Books present the information you need to learn about your report subject. In addition, they show you where to go on the Internet for more information. The pre-evaluated Report Links, listed on **www.myreportlinks.com**, save hours of research time and link to dozens—even hundreds—of Web sites, source documents, and photos related to your report topic.

To Our Readers:
Each Report Link has been reviewed by our editors, who will work hard to keep only active and appropriate Internet addresses in our books and up to date on our Web site. However, the author and the Publisher have no control over, and assume no liability for, the material available on those Internet sites, or on other Web sites they may link to.

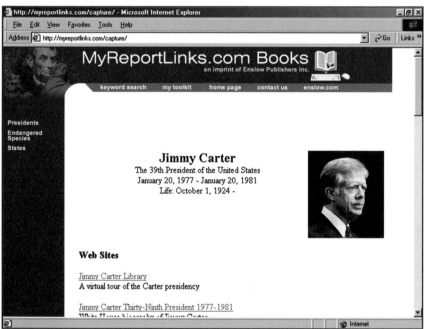

Access:
The Publisher will try to keep the Report Links that back up this book up to date on our Web site for three years from the book's first publication date. Please enter **PCA1932** if asked for a password.

Report Links

 The Internet sites described below can be accessed at
http://www.myreportlinks.com

*EDITOR'S CHOICE

▶ **Jimmy Carter Library**
A visit to the Carter Library brings the years of the Carter presidency
to life. The exhibits include details of Carter's daily activities in the
White House from 1977 through 1981, as well as copies of all his
major speeches.

Link to this Internet site from http://www.myreportlinks.com

*EDITOR'S CHOICE

▶ **Jimmy Carter, Thirty-Ninth President 1977–1981**
The official White House Web site provides a profile of U.S.
presidents. This page features a biography of Jimmy Carter, where you
can learn about Carter's aspirations for government and his
achievements as a human rights advocate.

Link to this Internet site from http://www.myreportlinks.com

*EDITOR'S CHOICE

▶ **Jimmy Carter: The Outsider President**
This comprehensive biography of Jimmy Carter provides basic facts
about Carter in addition to a detailed profile about his life before,
during, and after his presidency.

Link to this Internet site from http://www.myreportlinks.com

*EDITOR'S CHOICE

▶ **The American Presidency**
At this site you will find objects related all the presidents of the United
States, including Jimmy Carter. You can also read a brief description of
the era he lived in and learn about the office of the presidency.

Link to this Internet site from http://www.myreportlinks.com

*EDITOR'S CHOICE

▶ **James E. (Jimmy) Carter, Jr.**
At the hall of Public Service you will find a brief profile of Jimmy
Carter, a biography detailing his life before and after his presidency, and
a two-page interview covering his life and achievements.

Link to this Internet site from http://www.myreportlinks.com

*EDITOR'S CHOICE

▶ **The Camp David Accords**
Go on a virtual tour of Camp David! By navigating through this site
you can learn the history behind the Camp David Accords, read
President Carter's letter to Prime Minister Begin, and listen to an audio
recording of the key players.

Link to this Internet site from http://www.myreportlinks.com

Report Links

The Internet sites described below can be accessed at
http://www.myreportlinks.com

►America Votes: Jimmy Carter—1976/1980
From Duke University's "America Votes" collection of presidential campaign memorabilia come three items from the Carter campaigns of 1976 and 1980: two campaign buttons and a T-shirt with Carter's image.

Link to this Internet site from http://www.myreportlinks.com

►The American Presidency: Jimmy Carter
Part of Grolier's Multimedia American President series, this site offers a profile of Jimmy Carter and his presidency. In particular you will learn about Carter's naval service and his views on racism.

Link to this Internet site from http://www.myreportlinks.com

►The American Presidency: Walter F. Mondale
Grolier presents a brief biography of Jimmy Carter's vice president, Walter Mondale. This biography highlights Mondale's active role in the Carter administration and his service to Carter as a foreign affairs advisor.

Link to this Internet site from http://www.myreportlinks.com

►An Hour Before Daylight: Memories of a Rural Boyhood
On this page you can read a review of and a chapter from Jimmy Carter's memoir: *An Hour Before Daylight: Memories of a Rural Boyhood.*

Link to this Internet site from http://www.myreportlinks.com

►Booknotes Transcript
In February 1995, shortly after the release of his book *Always a Reckoning and Other Poems,* Jimmy Carter appeared on C-SPAN's popular Booknotes program. This is a transcript of his remarks about the just-published book of poetry.

Link to this Internet site from http://www.myreportlinks.com

►The Carter Center
Headquartered in Atlanta, Georgia, the Carter Center was founded by Jimmy and Rosalynn Carter. The Carter Center advocates human rights and peace throughout the world. This site provides a detailed examination of the organization's activities and goals.

Link to this Internet site from http://www.myreportlinks.com

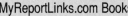
Report Links

 The Internet sites described below can be accessed at
http://www.myreportlinks.com

▶ **The Crisis of Confidence**
This page contains Jimmy Carter's speech "Crisis of Confidence,"
which was delivered on July 15, 1979. In the speech, Carter outlines
his proposal for a new energy program.

Link to this Internet site from http://www.myreportlinks.com

▶ **History Professor Assesses the Carter Presidency**
This site provides an interesting assessment of Carter's presidency from
a group of historians and biographers who discussed this presidency at
an Atlanta, Georgia, conference in 1997.

Link to this Internet site from http://www.myreportlinks.com

▶ **Infoplease.com: James Earl Carter Jr.**
Infoplease.com traces Jimmy Carter's rise from being a peanut farmer
in southern Georgia to his 1977 inauguration as president. Moreover,
you will learn of Carter's most notable achievements while in office.

Link to this Internet site from http://www.myreportlinks.com

▶ **James Earl Carter Jr.**
Part of Internet Public Library's POTUS (Presidents of the United
States) series, this site provides a quick-reference guide to the life and
times of the thirty-ninth president and offers links to the members of
his government.

Link to this Internet site from http://www.myreportlinks.com

▶ **James Earl Carter Jr. (1924–)**
This site holds the text of Jimmy Carter's inaugural address, delivered
on January 20, 1977, as well as his annual State of the Union addresses.

Link to this Internet site from http://www.myreportlinks.com

▶ **Jimmy Carter and Habitat**
Former President Jimmy Carter and his wife, Rosalynn, devote a week
of their time every year to a Habitat for Humanity construction project
somewhere in the world. Learn more about the Carters' involvement
with that program.

Link to this Internet site from http://www.myreportlinks.com

Report Links

▶**Jimmy Carter: Inaugural Address**
Bartleby.com's vast electronic library holds the text of Jimmy Carter's inaugural address. Delivered on January 20, 1977, Carter expressed his thanks to Gerald Ford for healing the country's wounds in the aftermath of Watergate.

Link to this Internet site from http://www.myreportlinks.com

▶**Jimmy Carter, January 20, 1977-January 20, 1981**
During the four years of his presidency, Jimmy Carter traveled extensively, visiting every continent except Antarctica and Australia. This site provides a list of all the foreign trips made by Carter while he was in the White House.

Link to this Internet site from http://www.myreportlinks.com

▶**Just for Kids!**
This site is designed especially for kids. Here you will find useful links, fun games, and a timeline filled with photographs.

Link to this Internet site from http://www.myreportlinks.com

▶**Newsmaker: President Carter: September 19, 1997**
Since leaving the White House, Jimmy Carter has, among other things, worked with African leaders to help improve farming techniques in their regions. On this page you will find a transcript of a PBS interview with Carter and his involvement in the project.

Link to this Internet site from http://www.myreportlinks.com

▶**Person of the Year**
For the past seventy years, *Time* magazine has bestowed its Person of the Year award to the individual of the past year it deemed the most influential. In 1976, the award was presented to Jimmy Carter. Read the *Time* article here.

Link to this Internet site from http://www.myreportlinks.com

▶**Plains, Georgia: Home of the 39th President of the United States**
Jimmy and Rosalynn Carter grew up in and around Plains, Georgia. As you will learn from this site, their ties to Plains remain strong. Visit this site to sample some of the down-home flavors of the Carters' hometown.

Link to this Internet site from http://www.myreportlinks.com

Report Links

The Internet sites described below can be accessed at
http://www.myreportlinks.com

▶ **Presidential Candidate Jimmy Carter speaks of growing up behind an "Invisible Wall of Racial Segregation," in Los Angeles, CA June 1, 1976.**
On this page you will read a campaign speech given by Jimmy Carter in Los Angeles, California, on June 1, 1976.

Link to this Internet site from http://www.myreportlinks.com

▶ **President Jimmy Carter**
From ThinkQuest comes a comprehensive biography of Jimmy Carter, featuring an audio clip of Carter's 1977 inaugural address. Carter's call for morality in government appealed to voters.

Link to this Internet site from http://www.myreportlinks.com

▶ **Rosalynn Smith Carter 1927–**
The official White House Web site provides a brief profile of United States First Ladies. This page contains biographical information about Rosalynn Carter and details about her work in the White House and her commitment to human rights.

Link to this Internet site from http://www.myreportlinks.com

▶ **SALT II Treaty**
This is the text of the SALT II Treaty signed in June 1979 by President Carter and Soviet Premier Leonid Brezhnev. Carter withdrew it from Senate consideration in early 1980, but the two countries adhered to its terms.

Link to this Internet site from http://www.myreportlinks.com

▶ **What Makes Jimmy Run?**
Fifteen years after Carter left office, *Life* magazine interviewed him. This article highlights many of Carter's undertakings since leaving the White House.

Link to this Internet site from http://www.myreportlinks.com

▶ **World Hello Day Letters: Jimmy Carter**
World Hello Day is an organization whose objective is to promote peace and communication globally between individuals and world leaders. This effort began as a result of the conflict between Israel and Egypt in 1973. This page features Jimmy Carter's letter.

Link to this Internet site from http://www.myreportlinks.com

Highlights

1924—*Oct. 1:* James Earl Carter is born on a peanut farm in Archery, Georgia.

1943—Carter is accepted to the U.S. Naval Academy in Annapolis, Maryland.

1946—Graduates from the U.S. Naval Academy.

Marries Rosalynn Smith.

1953—His father dies of cancer.

1962—Runs for the Georgia Senate. Wins the election and serves two terms.

1966—Runs for governor and loses the election.

1970—Runs for governor and wins the election.

1976—Runs for president against Gerald Ford and wins the election.

1977—*Jan. 20:* Inaugural Parade.

1978—*Sept.:* Peace talks at Camp David. Carter helps Egyptian president Anwar Sadat and Israeli leader Menachem Begin reach an agreement.

Congress passes the National Energy Act.

1979—*March:* Israeli settlers begin their withdrawal from the Sinai desert.

Nuclear breakdown occurs at Three Mile Island in Pennsylvania.

1980—Soviet General Secretary Leonid Brezhnev stations troops in Afghanistan. Carter demands that he remove the troops, but Brezhnev refuses. As a result, Carter pulls the United States out of the Summer Olympic Games, which were to be held in Moscow. Sixty-three other nations also did the same.

Fifty-two United States citizens held hostage by terrorists at the American Embassy in Tehran, Iran.

Carter loses presidential election to Ronald Reagan.

1981—*Jan. 20:* Hostages are released.

Jan.: Carter and his wife, Rosalynn, establish the Carter Center, an organization that promotes human rights, democracy, and health around the world.

1982—Carter and his wife engage in activities with Habitat for Humanity, a volunteer group that builds homes for people who cannot afford to buy them.

1998—Co-authors an article for the *New York Times* with Former President Ford concerning President Clinton's impeachment trial.

Chapter 1

The Fight for Peace, 1978

"Sadat is leaving!"[1]

President Jimmy Carter turned in his chair and faced Cyrus Vance, the man who had delivered the news. Leave? If Sadat left, every minute of the past eleven days would crumble to waste!

"He and his aides are already packed," Vance, America's secretary of defense, explained. "He asked me to order him a helicopter."[2]

President Carter gazed at the window and across the grounds of Camp David, Maryland. This is a place where presidents come to relax. Yet Carter had not relaxed for nearly two weeks. He had put aside almost every duty of his job as president to work with two leaders from the Middle East: Egyptian President Anwar Sadat and Israeli leader Menachem Begin. Now it seemed that the possibility of peace was about to disappear.

▶ Long-Standing War

Israel and Egypt are both countries in the Middle East. This area of the world is well-known for producing oil and also for violent religious wars. The problems between Sadat and Begin's nations were long-standing and complicated, centering around an area called Palestine. Both Arabs (which included Egyptians) and Jews had lived in Palestine for centuries. Over the centuries, Palestine had been governed by many groups of people. After World War I, Great Britain was granted control of Palestine by the League of Nations. Meanwhile, during the 1920s, 1930s, and 1940s, relations between the Jewish and Arab settlers in Palestine grew heated. In November 1947, the United Nations decided to split Palestine between the Jews and Arabs. That lasted only six months. Britain's control over Palestine was scheduled to end in May 1948, and when it did, the State of Israel declared itself to be a nation. It was unusual for a group of people—in this case, the Jews—to create a new nation on land that was already inhabited by other people. This angered the Arabs, who felt like their land had been stolen from them. The result has been decades of bloody war. During one of those wars—in 1967—Israel seized lands that were held by the Arabs. Those areas (the Sinai Peninsula, Golan Heights, West Bank, and Gaza Strip) became points of contention between the Jews and Arabs.

Carter wanted to take steps to end that fighting. So, he convinced both Sadat and Begin to join him for peace talks at Camp David in September 1978. Everybody involved planned to be there for only a few days. Soon, it became clear that nothing could be accomplished in such a short time. In fact, any time Begin and Sadat were in the same room, they would begin arguing. Carter found that it worked better for him to meet with each man separately, going back and forth between the two to share ideas.

Even after a week and a half, it seemed as if little substantial progress had been made. The sticking point was the issue of Jewish people living in Egypt's Sinai Peninsula. Sadat wanted those people to move out of the desert land. Begin simply would not agree to order his people out. Frustrated, Sadat decided it was time to leave for home.

▶ Saving Peace

After Secretary Vance told Carter about Sadat's plans to leave, the president remained silent for several minutes. He said a prayer. Carter knew that what he was about to do would be recorded forever in history. When his mind was set, Carter walked out of his cabin, across the grounds of Camp David, and into another cabin. Among several packed bags stood the Egyptian president. Carter faced Sadat and told him that if he left, America's good relationship with Egypt would be harmed. And that was not all: If Sadat left, Carter said, their personal friendship would be seriously hurt. Impressively, Carter convinced Sadat to stay.

Things still did not flow smoothly. Prime Minister Begin remained unwilling to budge on the issue of ordering Jewish settlers out of the Sinai desert. In fact, Carter had found Begin difficult to work with throughout their entire stay at Camp David. In his book, *Talking Peace*, Carter wrote that Begin had "become quite unfriendly toward me because of the pressure I was putting on him and Sadat."[3] But two days after convincing Sadat to stay, Carter had a breakthrough with Begin.

On day thirteen, Carter delivered to Begin some signed photographs of the three leaders. Carter had personalized each of his autographs to Begin's grandchildren with their names. As Begin read the names aloud, he began to think about how important peace was to saving lives and families. He agreed to leave the issue of the Jewish settlers to the Knesset, Israel's parliament. If the Knesset voted to move the settlers, they would go. If not, they would stay. Sadat agreed to this compromise.

Finally, a peace agreement was reached. Begin and Sadat shook hands at Camp David, then everyone boarded

http://www.sowega.net/~plainsed/kidsite/kidimages/handshake.jpg - Microsoft Internet Explorer

File   Edit   View   Favorites   Tools   Help

Address http://www.sowega.net/~plainsed/kidsite/kidimages/handshake.jpg   Go   Links

Done   Internet

▲ *At Camp David, President Carter helped two leaders from the Middle East peacefully settle a dispute. Carter smiles as he grasps the hands of Egyptian President Anwar Sadat, left, and Israeli Prime Minister Menachem Begin, right, at the Egyptian-Israeli Peace Treaty signing.*

helicopters to fly back to the White House for the signing ceremony. Six months later, in March 1979, Israeli settlers had begun their withdrawal. A formal treaty was signed between Israel and Egypt, again at the White House. With Sadat on his right and Begin to the left, Carter clasped the hands of the two former enemies.

Jimmy Carter, a man who one decade earlier had been a peanut farmer, had just sealed an agreement that could save thousands of lives. He was president of the United States, but more importantly at that moment, Carter was a peacemaker for the world.

Chapter 2

Growing Up, 1924–1942

When he was six, Jimmy Carter had a simple way of telling good people from bad. The good people, he thought, were ones who bought peanuts from him. The bad ones were those who did not.

▶ Growing Up on the Farm

James Earl Carter was born on October 1, 1924. He grew up on a farm in Archery, Georgia. By age six, Jimmy had learned to make use of his dad's peanut crop. Jimmy picked the nuts, boiled them in salt water and bagged them. He walked three miles down the railroad tracks to the nearby town of Plains and sold the bags for a nickel apiece.

Jimmy had about ten regular customers. On a normal day, Jimmy's peanut sales earned him one dollar. Most of that money he saved. Although, sometimes he did treat himself to an ice cream cone. In town, he could often be seen playing a game of checkers or spinning tops.

Jimmy occasionally played jokes on his younger siblings: Gloria, Ruth, and Billy. Though he was usually playing outside or absorbed in a book, Jimmy could get into a little mischief. He would then learn his lessons after a brief punishment.

A strict, hard-working man, Jimmy's father, Earl Carter, was a successful farmer and smart businessman. Jimmy's mother, Lillian, was a registered nurse who gave a lot of her time toward treating African Americans whom white doctors often refused to see.

Back   Forward   Stop   Review   Home   Explore   Favorites   History

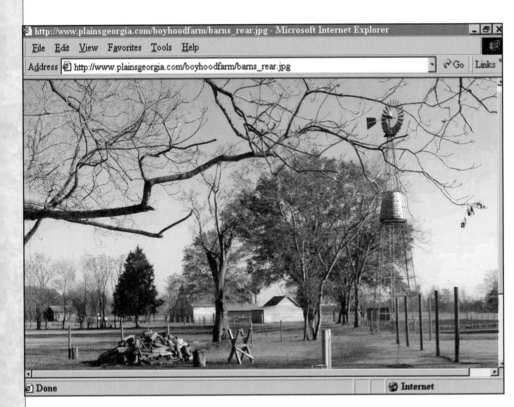

http://www.plainsgeorgia.com/boyhoodfarm/barns_rear.jpg - Microsoft Internet Explorer

File   Edit   View   Favorites   Tools   Help

Address   http://www.plainsgeorgia.com/boyhoodfarm/barns_rear.jpg   Go   Links

Done   Internet

▲ *The Carter family peanut farm in Archery, Georgia. As a young boy, Jimmy bagged the peanuts and walked three miles down the road to Plains, where he sold the bags for a nickel a piece.*

The Carters lived in a wooden house heated by two fireplaces and a woodstove. They did not have indoor plumbing until Jimmy was eleven, and there was not any electricity until he was fourteen. When the electricity was installed, both Miss Lillian and the kids were thrilled that they were now able to read after sunset. Television was a few decades away, but the Carters did have one battery-powered radio on their porch that occasionally got reception late at night.

School Days

Jimmy's favorite teacher was Miss Julia Coleman. She was the principal, and taught several grades at her school in Plains. Coleman had her students memorize the names and works of great artists and composers. She encouraged them to memorize and recite poems. Most importantly, she inspired Jimmy to read. When he was twelve, she convinced him to read Tolstoy's *War and Peace*, a 1,400-page book. Jimmy loved it so much that he reread it three or four times as an adult. Miss Julia made her students love learning. Many years later, when Jimmy Carter became

▲ James Earl Carter was a strict father who stressed the importance of discipline and hard work to his children. Pictured with him from left are Ruth, Gloria, and Jimmy.

http://www.plainsgeorgia.com/boyhoodfarm/back_porch.jpg - Microsoft Internet Explorer

File   Edit   View   Favorites   Tools   Help

Address http://www.plainsgeorgia.com/boyhoodfarm/back_porch.jpg   Go   Links

Done   Internet

▲ *When Jimmy was young, there was no electricity, heat, or indoor plumbing in his home. The Carters heated bricks in the oven, wrapped them in cloth, and then placed them in their beds for warmth.*

president, he often told people just how much Miss Julia had influenced him. He even mentioned her in his inaugural speech.

Jimmy went to school with all white children in Plains. The law back then stated that whites and blacks were educated separately. The problem was, African Americans almost never got equal treatment. Jimmy hated that. Back home in Archery, most of his friends were African American. One of his best buddies was A. D. Davis. They did all sorts of fun things together, from skinny-dipping in ponds, to flying homemade kites, to riding around on Earl Carter's bull calf when no one was watching.

▶ Civil Rights

One day when they went to see a movie, Jimmy wanted A. D. to sit with him in the downstairs section that was reserved for white people. When A. D. sat down, he quickly noticed white customers getting upset, so he went upstairs to the black seats. Jimmy would not stand for it; he wanted his friend downstairs. They both ended up leaving. Things like that happened more than once.

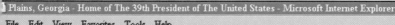

More than any President in recent years, Jimmy Carter is closely identified with his hometown. Americans marvel at how a man from such isolated, small-town upbringing came to broaden his horizons to eventually aspire to the highest office in the country. Even his hometown people were surprised by his decision to seek the Presidency

``It was a little shocking that someone we knew wanted to be the President. Why not?'' said Mrs. Maxine Reese, campaign manager at the Plains headquarters.

Why not, indeed! The townspeople of Plains rolled up their sleeves and eagerly set to work to help elect their native son to the Presidency. The Democratic National Committee was thrilled when the town of Plains put on a covered dish campaign dinner that raised one million dollars, the most ever raised at a single fundraising event. Hometown support was obvious when an eighteen-car passenger train dubbed the ``Peanut Express (Special),'' departed from the Plains depot filled to capacity with ecstatic passengers bound for the 39th Presidential

▲ This is a schoolhouse similar to the one Jimmy attended. In the 1930s, schools such as this one lacked the funds necessary to make improvements. His experience at this school gave Carter the incentive to improve education.

Though slavery had been abolished over fifty years earlier, black people still lived in different neighborhoods than whites, attended separate schools, and sat in restricted seats in public places. Blacks were supposed to address whites as "Mr." and "Miss," but whites did not have to show equal respect for blacks. This was true moreso in the southern United States.

"Don't know as I'm ever going to start calling you 'Mr. Jimmy,'" A. D. told Jimmy one day. "I wouldn't blame you," Jimmy answered. "I wouldn't either."[1]

Two of the most important people in Jimmy's life were an African-American couple, Jack and Rachel Clark. The Clarks lived on the Carter farm and worked in the cotton fields. Jack sometimes took Jimmy raccoon hunting and taught him how to plow with a mule and milk cows. Rachel Clark took Jimmy fishing in the swamp, and out into the cotton field. The two would have friendly cotton-picking competitions to see who could pick more. The loser would have to carry all of the cotton in. Rachel always won, Jimmy usually carried the cotton. "He couldn't pick as much as me," Rachel remembered years later. "He just picked. He tried."[2]

When Earl and Lillian would leave town for work or vacation, Jimmy would stay in the small woodshed that was Jack and Rachel's home. His bed was a small piece of padding in a corner on the floor, but he loved being there. "I felt just as much at home in Rachel and Jack's house as I did in my house," Jimmy said many years later.[3]

Being so close with Jack and Rachel Clark allowed Jimmy to see the differences between how blacks and whites were treated. Years later, whether on the farm or in the White House, those were lessons he would always remember.

Chapter 3 ▶

Rising to the Presidency, 1943–1972

While Jimmy Carter was growing up, he always looked forward to receiving postcards from his uncle, who traveled the world with the United States Navy. By age six, Jimmy knew he wanted to join the Navy as well.

It was the first of many big dreams that he made come true. He took classes at a couple of Georgia colleges. Soon, he was accepted to the U.S. Naval Academy in Annapolis, Maryland, in 1943. The first year was difficult. All the freshmen endured "hazing," a rough, sometimes cruel initiation from the older students. Things got better after that. Carter earned good grades and even participated in track and football.

▶ The Girl I Want to Marry

During the summer vacation before his senior year, Carter was driving around Plains in a Ford with his friend. The two young men saw Carter's younger sister, Ruth, and her friend Rosalynn Smith in the churchyard. She was three years younger than him and, after all, she was his little sister's friend! But on this summer day, Jimmy found

In this photo from 1945, ▶ Jimmy expresses his love for Rosalynn. The couple was married a year later.

▲ *On the day of his graduation from the U.S. Naval Academy, fiancée Rosalynn Smith and mother Lillian Carter attach Ensign bars to the shoulders of Carter's uniform.*

that he liked Rosalynn very much. He kissed her that very night and when he returned home, told his mom, "She's the girl I want to marry."[1]

His wish was granted. Jimmy and Rosalynn wed on July 7, 1946, shortly after his graduation from Annapolis.

▶ In the Navy

Jimmy and Rosalynn's first home was a small apartment in Norfolk, Virginia. There, Jimmy had been assigned to the battleship *Mississippi*. The Carters' first son, Jack, was born in 1947. Over the next six years, Jimmy and Rosalynn would move several times. In Connecticut, Jimmy Carter was trained as a submarine officer, then assigned to

Hawaii, where their son Chip was born. Four years later they moved back to Connecticut, then to Schenectady, New York, where Carter was helping develop a new nuclear submarine.

By this time the Carters had three children. Their third son, Jeffrey, had been born in Connecticut. Jimmy Carter had a promising career in the Navy. At age twenty-eight, Lieutenant Carter was being trained in nuclear physics and was on a path to one day become an admiral.

Returning Home

Lieutenant Carter's life changed drastically one day in 1953. He received a phone call that his father was dying of cancer. The Navy allowed Jimmy Carter to leave with Rosalynn and the kids to drive home and say goodbye. When Earl died, the public grief was great. People filled the parking lot and yard of the Plains Baptist Church for his funeral. Seeing how much his father meant to the community, Carter began thinking hard. He felt a need to take his father's place, not only in running the family business, but as a leading citizen in Plains, too.

After a lot of thinking, Carter quit the Navy. Rosalynn was angry. She knew how hard her husband had worked and how promising his military career was. She also realized that there was no stopping him from going home. So the Carters left the military behind and returned to an apartment in Plains. Carter returned to his first-ever job: peanut farming. He also ran Carter's Warehouse, which sold farm goods and supplies.

Political Aspirations

Like his father, Carter was interested in politics. While Earl tended to have more conservative views, Jimmy was more

http://www.sowega.net/~plainsed/kidsite/kidimages/public.jpg - Microsoft Internet Explorer

File   Edit   View   Favorites   Tools   Help

Address http://www.sowega.net/~plainsed/kidsite/kidimages/public.jpg   Go   Links

Done   Internet

When his father died of cancer, Jimmy Carter moved his family back to Plains, Georgia. Due to limited income, the family had to live in apartment 9A of this public housing unit.

liberal, like his mother, Lillian. Education was important to him, so he joined the county school board and became chairman. Carter also joined the Georgia Planning Committee and became the group's first president. He made some tough choices, too. When a group of men were forming a White Citizens Council to keep the blacks and whites separate in Plains, they asked Carter to join. He said no, and became the only white man in Plains not to join. People became angry and Carter's Warehouse lost customers, but Jimmy stuck to his beliefs.

Run for Office

In 1962, Carter decided to run for the Georgia Senate. On election day, it first appeared that Carter had lost. Then, a newspaper reporter discovered that the Republican chairman had cheated to fix the election. A court ordered a new vote. This time, Carter won and became a state senator.

Carter enjoyed working on the state level for issues in which he really believed: education, mental health, consumer reform, and civil rights. He spoke out against the "30 Questions Test." This was a nearly-impossible test

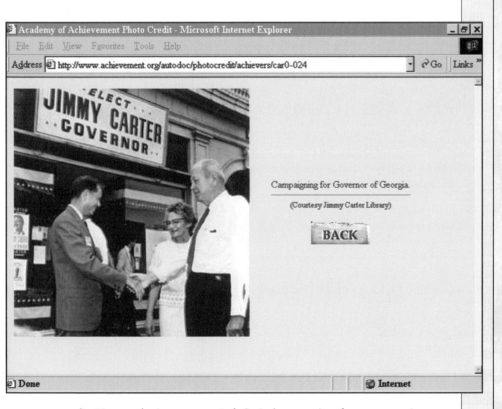

Academy of Achievement Photo Credit - Microsoft Internet Explorer

File   Edit   View   Favorites   Tools   Help

Address http://www.achievement.org/autodoc/photocredit/achievers/car0-024   Go   Links

Campaigning for Governor of Georgia

(Courtesy Jimmy Carter Library)

BACK

Done   Internet

▲ Many volunteers supported Carter's campaign for governor in 1970. During his term as governor, Carter accomplished important goals, such as improving the environment, and organizing a group to help alleviate racial tensions.

used by election officials in some Georgia counties to discourage African Americans from voting.

In 1966, after two Senate terms, Carter lost a run for governor. Suddenly, he was out of politics. In church one day shortly after his defeat, Jimmy heard the preacher say, "If you were arrested for being a Christian, would there be enough evidence to convict you?"[2] He decided to focus more on God and religion in his life. Not long after, in 1967, Rosalynn gave birth to the Carters' fourth child, Amy. Excited about his newfound faith and baby daughter, Jimmy Carter decided to run for governor again in 1970. This time, by running an organized campaign with the help of his wife and sons, Carter was elected.

As governor, Carter cleaned up Georgia's government, getting rid of unnecessary programs that wasted taxpayers' money. Health care, education and the environment were among his top priorities. So was equality. Governor Carter got more African Americans and women involved in high-level government jobs. He hung a picture of Reverend Martin Luther King, Jr., in the Georgia State Capitol and in his inaugural speech declared that the time for discrimination was over. "No poor, rural, weak, or black person should ever have to bear the additional burden of being deprived of the opportunity of an education, a job, or simple justice."[3]

Chapter 4

Election to the White House, 1973–1976

One evening in 1973, Jimmy Carter visited his mother in her room at the Governor's mansion. Miss Lillian had taught her children to chase the loftiest goals no matter how out of reach they seemed. That was the way she lived her own life. In the late 1960s, at age sixty-eight, Miss Lillian had traveled to the poorest part of India as a Peace Corps volunteer nurse for two years. But even Miss Lillian was surprised when her son told her he was going to run for president. "President of what?" she asked.[1]

▶ The Outsider

The United States, of course. Having been a governor, Carter felt he was qualified for the job. So in 1976, he found himself running against current Republican President Gerald Ford. Ford had replaced the disgraced former president, Richard Nixon. Some people who worked for Nixon had authorized a break-in at the Democratic National Headquarters in Washington's Watergate office building. After he took office in 1974, Ford had pardoned Nixon from facing any charges in the Watergate scandal. It had been learned that Nixon knew of the break-in himself and allegedly tried to cover it up. With Ford's pardon, he would not have to face any legal charges. Many Americans, however, were outraged. They felt Nixon should have to stand trial just like any other citizen.

So by 1976, when Ford was running for election, the mood of the country was perfectly tuned for someone new

to national politics. Carter traveled around the country pointing out that he was not from Washington, that he had never worked in the nation's capital, and would not do any favors for old friends.

People listened. For a little less than a year, Carter and Ford waged a hard-fought campaign. Ford and his aides pointed out that Carter had no experience in Washington. For that reason, they said, he was not best-qualified to be president. "Why are we going to win?" said Ron Nessen, Ford's press secretary. "I just sense it. It's really come down to the character of the two men, there's no really big issue moving people to vote one way or another. It's which man the voters feel more comfortable with."[2] Carter did invoke a hot issue into the campaign, reminding voters that Ford was the man who pardoned Nixon. To get some Washington experience on his side, Carter picked Minnesota Senator Walter "Fritz" Mondale as his vice presidential running mate.

On election day in November 1976, Carter won 50 percent of the popular vote; Ford won 48 percent. With 297 electoral votes to Ford's 240, Carter won the presidency.

▶ The Walk To Washington

From the beginning, Jimmy Carter proved that he would be a different kind of president. During his inaugural parade in January 1977, the president and first lady, along with daughter Amy, walked down Pennsylvania Avenue to the White House instead of taking the traditional ride in a limousine. During his inaugural speech, President Carter made a rare gesture: He thanked President Ford, the man he had just beat. "For myself and for our nation, I want to

Tools · Search · Notes · Discuss · Go!

America Votes: Jimmy Carter - Microsoft Internet Explorer

File   Edit   View   Favorites   Tools   Help

Address 🔗 http://scriptorium.lib.duke.edu/americavotes/carter.html   ▾   ⟳ Go   Links »

America Votes
Presidential Campaign Memorabilia from the Duke University Special Collections
Library

Jimmy Carter - 1976/1980

[Larger version of this item]

🔵 Internet

▲ *In his 1976 presidential campaign, Carter had to convince Americans that he was qualified to be president. The "Jimmy Carter: Not Just Peanuts" slogan appeared on posters, buttons, and other items.*

thank my predecessor for all he has done to heal our country," Carter said, turning to shake Ford's hand.[3]

In the White House, President Carter kept a busy schedule, sometimes working as many as sixteen hours per day. His days typically began around half past six in the morning, when he would take an hour to read the newspaper, write letters or fill out paperwork. Around 7:30 A.M., meetings would begin. Often they lasted well into the night.

▲ *Rather than riding in a limousine, Carter walked in the Inaugural Day Parade with his wife and daughter.*

▶ The First Family

When Carter did have some time alone with his family, he preferred the White House cooks to serve up southern dishes such as grits, peanut soup, country ham, corn bread and Georgia peach cobbler. The president liked to relax by playing tennis, bowling, skiing, bicycling, and jogging.

For Amy Carter, being the first daughter was not easy. On her first day of school at Stevens Elementary in Washington, she was late because her motorcade got held up in rush hour traffic. That would not be a big deal, except her tardiness made national news. Secret Service agents traveled to school with her everyday. Obviously, she was the only fourth grader with bodyguards.

As first lady, Rosalynn Carter spoke out on issues that were important to her, including mental health programs and equal rights for women. As a young woman, Rosalynn

Tools   Search   Notes   Discuss   Go!

Carter had been shy. She did not like to give long speeches in front of big crowds. When her husband was running for governor of Georgia, Mrs. Carter worked hard at overcoming her shyness so she could help him campaign.

Now, as first lady, she sometimes joined the president for Cabinet meetings and traveled to foreign countries. She even testified to Congress to gain support for mental health programs. Mrs. Carter was the only First Lady to have spoken to Congress since Eleanor Roosevelt. Jimmy Carter faced many challenges and much criticism as president. The one person always by his side was Rosalynn.

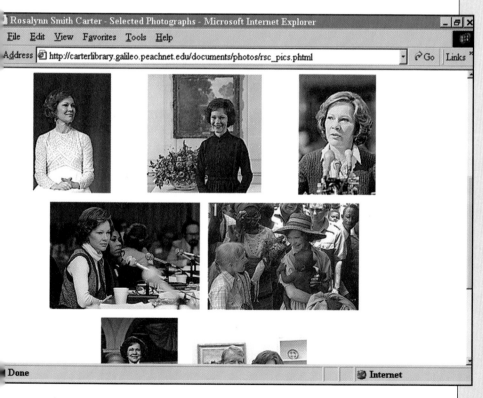

Rosalynn Smith Carter - Selected Photographs - Microsoft Internet Explorer

File   Edit   View   Favorites   Tools   Help

Address   http://carterlibrary.galileo.peachnet.edu/documents/photos/rsc_pics.phtml   Go   Links

Done   Internet

▲ First Lady Rosalynn Carter sometimes accompanied her husband on trips to foreign lands and supported him when he faced criticism. Rosalynn also spoke out on issues that were important to her, such as equal rights for women and developing programs for the mentally challenged.

Chapter 5

Issues in Office, 1976–1980

Three months after he was sworn into office, President Carter received a letter from a woman in Los Angeles, California. "I voted for you," she wrote. "I think that the main reason that I voted for you was because where I saw Mr. Ford had an open mind I saw that you had an open heart. I feel that God can work more through an open heart."[1]

The woman wrote on to say that she was sure Carter wanted to make not only America, but the world, a better place. One week later, the president wrote back. The body of the letter was a form message received by thousands of people who wrote to the president every week. But at the bottom, Carter added a handwritten postscript: "I'll try to keep my open heart!"[2]

Carter never broke that promise. He always followed his beliefs, even when they were unpopular.

▶ Saving Energy

Carter hated waste. Growing up, he had been expected to eat every bit of food on his dinner plate. He had also lived in a house heated by two fireplaces and a wood stove. So when he realized that Americans were using too much natural gas and oil to heat their homes and operate their cars, he asked the country for a favor. Dressed in a sweater, sitting in front of a crackling fire, Carter smiled into a television camera and asked Americans to turn their thermostats down to 65°F during the day, and 55°F at

▲ When Americans faced an energy crisis in the late 1970s, Carter introduced an energy plan. Despite a loss in popularity with oil and gas companies and automobile manufacturers, Carter refused to give in to big industries. Congress passed his National Energy Act in 1978.

night. He explained that the costs of oil and gas were rising too high and Americans were using too much. The Organization of Petroleum Exporting Countries (OPEC) had raised oil prices to astronomical levels. Carter felt that America's best solution was to consume less.

At this, oil and gas companies in the United States grew angry. Such an energy plan would cause them to lose money. Automobile manufacturers did not like it either, because they would be required to spend money developing cars that used less gas. OPEC's high prices also eventually forced car companies to produce more fuel-efficient automobiles. Despite the opposition, Carter stuck to his plan and tried to convince congressional representatives to join

him. He won, but not convincingly: Congress passed a weakened version of the National Energy Act in 1978. Many historians believe that if Carter had more inside contacts in Congress, he could have pushed through a stronger version of the act.

Carter did not mind taking sides against big industries. Throughout his presidency he worked to preserve land for wildlife and national parks. In March 1979, he dealt with an environmental catastrophe when the nuclear plant at Three Mile Island in Harrisburg, Pennsylvania experienced a leakage. The breakdown led to stricter safety regulations for nuclear plants.

▶ Battling Prices

Carter had far less success battling rising prices of goods. This problem, called inflation, had been an issue during Ford's presidency. Now it was his problem. Prices were rising too high, too fast. For example, a bicycle that cost forty-four dollars in 1970 more than doubled in price to ninety-four dollars by 1980. People were not making enough money to keep up with the increasing prices.

To control inflation, Carter cut spending on government programs. He also deregulated, or got rid of some government rules, for companies that dealt in oil, gas, railroads, trucking, and air travel. None of the solutions worked, however.

▶ International Issues

Partly from his religious beliefs, and partly from the influence of his mother, President Carter cared deeply about people and world peace. That is why he put so much effort into bringing together Egyptian President Anwar Sadat and Israeli Prime Minister Menachem Begin.

▲ *President Jimmy Carter and Deputy Premier Deng Xiaoping of China shake hands, signaling an improvement in diplomatic relations between the two countries, which, until the early 1970s, had not communicated for twenty years.*

Wanting to show that the United States could deal fairly with smaller countries, Carter worked out a deal with Panama in 1977. By the year 2000, this Central American country would regain full control of the Panama Canal, which the United States had built in the early 1900s.

Building relationships with larger countries was important, too. Carter worked to strengthen the United States' relationship with a former enemy, Communist China.

▶ The Hotline

The angriest moment of Carter's presidency came in late 1979, when he picked up the hotline phone that connected the White House directly to the Kremlin in Moscow.

▲ *Soviet General Secretary Leonid Brezhnev and President Jimmy Carter signed the SALT II agreement on June 18, 1979. Despite efforts to maintain peace, however, the Soviet Union invaded Afghanistan in December of the same year. This caused more tension between the two nations.*

He called Soviet General Secretary Leonid Brezhnev and demanded that Soviet troops be pulled out of Afghanistan.

Brezhnev had sent thousands of soldiers to the smaller, neighboring country to quiet people who were protesting against the Soviet backed government there. Carter considered this to be a bully-like move by the Soviets, but Brezhnev did not budge. The troops stayed.

Carter protested by pulling the United States team out of the 1980 Summer Olympics, which were held in Moscow. Sixty-three other nations did the same. The Soviet invasion also killed a treaty Carter had agreed upon with Brezhnev to limit the development of nuclear arms.

Hostage Crisis

Carter won a tough battle with Senator Ted Kennedy for the Democratic nomination. Then, he faced the Republican ex-governor of California, Ronald Reagan, in the 1980 Presidential election. A former movie actor, Reagan had a knack for looking and sounding great on television. Later, as president, he would be nicknamed The Great Communicator.

Of course, Carter was president, which is usually an advantage—unless something is going wrong in the country. And in 1980, something was terribly wrong. At the American Embassy in Teheran, Iran, fifty-two United States citizens were being held hostage. A militant group was angry that the United States had shown hospitality to their enemy, the former leader of Iran, Shah Reza Pahlavi. The U.S. government had allowed the Shah to receive medical attention in New York before he went to Panama, and then Egypt. They wanted the Shah returned to Iran to stand trial. In exchange, the hostages would be released.

Carter would not simply give in to terrorists. He tried to peacefully negotiate the hostages' release, but that failed. He then tried to hurt Iran economically by stopping the importation of Iranian oil to the United States and freezing Iranian assets in the United States.

Finally, in April 1980, he dispatched a military rescue mission to seize the hostages. While landing in Iran, three of the helicopters broke down in a sandstorm. The mission was canceled, and while the aircraft began to evacuate, a helicopter crashed with a C-130 transport plane and killed eight American servicemen. Nothing seemed to be working. That mishap, more than any other, portrayed the United States as being militarily weak.

In addition to the hostage crisis, Carter was criticized for steep inflation and the high price of oil. Not even a president has the power to fix those problems alone, but Americans seemed to blame Carter for their woes. Being a Washington outsider did not help, either. Even though both the House and the Senate were controlled by Democrats, Carter had trouble rallying his fellow party members to support his ideas. Having no support from Congress—particularly when it is controlled by your own party—can render a president weak.

Another problem was Carter's reluctance to delegate power to his assistants and Cabinet members. When examining an issue or making a decision, Carter preferred to deal with the small details himself. During the Camp David peace talks, that worked. But typically, a president needs to surround himself with a tight circle of people whom he trusts to make some decisions for him. Carter, who fired several of his Cabinet members in 1979, never had that. By election night in November 1980, it was clear that Reagan would win the White House.

For his last two-and-a-half months in office, Carter devoted most of his time to gaining the release of the hostages. The Shah had died in July 1980 and the militants were under the control of the Iranian leader, Ayatollah Khomeini. In the last few days of his presidency, Carter worked around the clock for their release. Finally, on his last morning as president, an agreement was struck. The hostages were released on January 20, 1981, just as Ronald Reagan took the oath of office. One day after leaving Washington, Carter flew to Germany and welcomed the American hostages back to free soil.

Chapter 6 ▶

After the Presidency

Several years after they left the White House, Jimmy and Rosalynn Carter were eating dinner outside on a beautiful summer night with guests from the African countries of Ethiopia and Eritrea. For thirty years those two countries had been at war. On this evening, though, the enemies were smiling and relaxing as they worked on a peace agreement.

▶ Global Peacemaker

Then an airplane flew overhead. One of the Eritreans dropped to the ground and scurried under the table. Everyone else looked on, puzzled. The man quickly stood up and explained, "Please excuse me, but in my country when an airplane flies over, it drops bombs."[1]

Until the terrorist assaults on the World Trade Center and Pentagon on September 11, 2001, most Americans could never imagine hiding from an attacking aircraft. At any given moment approximately thirty wars are being fought around the world, most of them in countries so small that you almost never read about them in newspapers or magazines. As a former President of the United States, Jimmy Carter is one of the few people in the world with enough influence and knowledge to help stop these wars. That is why many historians consider Jimmy Carter to have accomplished more after leaving office than any other former president.

▶ Building A New Life

Jimmy Carter's new life as an ex-president began in January 1981. Though he was heartbroken to lose the White House, Carter did not get too discouraged. Instead, he spent the next year setting up the Carter Center, an organization that promotes human rights, democracy, and health around the world.

Working mostly with small countries and political groups, the Carter Center has tried to make life better in over one hundred nations. Peace agreements are not always reached, but that is alright. "Part of our mission is that failure is acceptable," said Dr. Joyce Neu, who is part of the Carter Center's conflict resolution program. "Not to try is not."[2]

▶ Traveling The World

President Carter and Mrs. Carter still make about a dozen overseas trips each year. Since leaving office, he has visited over 110 countries on behalf of the Carter Center. "Their schedules are extremely hectic: I've been here thirteen years and I haven't seen any sign of them slowing down," said Carrie Harmon, Carter's spokesperson, at the end of 2000.[3]

Every time President Carter makes a trip abroad, he uses his laptop computer on the plane ride home to write a detailed report. One of the people who receives this report is the current president. Typically, President and Mrs. Carter travel two weeks out of the month, spend one week at the Carter Center in Atlanta, and one week at home in Plains. As much as possible, President Carter tries to be in Plains on the weekends because he teaches Sunday School at Maranatha Baptist Church.

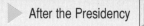

The Carter Center - Microsoft Internet Explorer

File　Edit　View　Favorites　Tools　Help

Address　http://www.cartercenter.org　　　Go　Links

THE CARTER CENTER

ABOUT US　PEACE PROGRAMS　HEALTH PROGRAMS　MEDIA CENTER　OUR FACILITIES　SUPPORT OUR WORK

FIGHTING DISEASE

Welcome to The Carter Center

Every day in countries all over the world, people live under difficult, life-threatening circumstances caused by war, disease, famine, and poverty. The non-profit Carter Center strives to relieve this suffering by advancing peace and health in neighborhoods and nations around the globe.

In the News...

Former U.S. President Jimmy Carter To Visit China (learn more)

Carter Center election reports and statements are now found on the individual country pages (learn more)

Carter Center Releases Preliminary Statement on East Timor Elections (learn more)

Click on above picture

The Center, in partnership with Emory University, is guided by a fundamental commitment to human rights, wages peace by bringing warring parties to the negotiating table, monitoring elections, safeguarding human rights, and building strong democracies through economic development.

It sows the seeds of peace in other ways--by fighting disease, increasing crop production, and

Done　　　　　　　　Internet

 After his term as president, Carter and his wife set up the Carter Center, a nonprofit organization designed to help people around the world who are suffering from disease, famine, and poverty.

In the years since he left the White House, one of Carter's best friends has been President Gerald Ford, the man he beat in the 1976 election. The two really did not like each other until 1981, when they found themselves together on an airplane flying home from President Anwar Sadat's funeral in Egypt. Carter and Ford found they agreed on many world issues and decided to work together whenever possible. Mrs. Carter and Mrs. Ford also became friends, and the relationship between the two presidential couples grew stronger over the next two decades.

Together in December 1998, Carter and Ford co-authored an article in *The New York Times* that

suggested a solution to President Clinton's impeachment trial. Since Carter is a Democrat and Ford is a Republican, their joint ideas are considered to be nonpartisan, or not political. After the controversial election of President George W. Bush in 2000, Carter and Ford oversaw a commission that studied ways to improve elections within the United States.

"They live on opposite ends of the country, so it's not like they get together for dinner every few weeks," said Harmon. "But they have a lot of shared interests, and they do talk a lot and communicate a lot . . . Even when they don't agree, they talk about issues. They just have a lot of respect for each other."[4]

Helping At Home

Though they live in the same house in Plains that they owned before Jimmy became governor, President and Mrs. Carter no longer own a farm or warehouse. The Carter boyhood home is now a national park, though the town of Archery no longer exists. It gradually disappeared as farmers moved away.

Atlanta is now like a second home to Jimmy and Rosalynn, who have an apartment at the Carter Center. One day Carter took a walk and noticed people living in shacks only a hundred yards away from his office on the lush grounds of the Center. Shocked and saddened, he wanted to help. Experiences like that prodded the Carters to develop a program called The Atlanta Project (TAP), which provides health care, education, housing, crime prevention programs, and legal services for the most needy. TAP has become a model for similar programs around the country.

Habitat For Humanity International: 1999 Jimmy Carter Work Project - Microsoft Internet Explorer

File   Edit   View   Favorites   Tools   Help

Address http://www.habitat.org/jcwp/99/mon1.html   Go   Links »

Jimmy Carter Work Project 1999

Done   Internet

▲ Since his retirement from the presidency, Jimmy and
Rosalynn Carter have been actively involved in Habitat
for Humanity. Here they are pictured with two thousand
other volunteers at the Maragondon building site.

Aside from their Carter Center work, Jimmy and
Rosalynn keep busy by writing books. President Carter
has written fifteen books, including his White House
memoirs, a poetry book, a children's picture book, and an
autobiography about growing up in the south. Together,
President and Mrs. Carter have written books about
how people can make good with their lives while
growing older.

One of most visible ways President and Mrs. Carter
have done that is by building homes with Habitat for

Humanity. This organization builds houses for people who cannot afford to buy them. Since they became involved in 1982, President and Mrs. Carter have built a Habitat home each year and helped raise money for the organization.

▶ A Good Neighbor

Carter has never been shy about pointing out problems that need fixing, even in his hometown. During a visit to an Atlanta middle school, he had a conversation with a student that he will never forget.

"Mr. President," a girl asked him, "why do old people lose their Social Security?" "Honey," Carter answered, "old people don't lose their Social Security. They get it unless their income goes up." "I think you're wrong, Mr. President," she said. "My granddaddy lost his Social Security. He didn't have no income. He lives under a bridge and lost it because he didn't have no mailing address."[5] After talking with this girl, Carter spoke with a Social Security official who agreed to fix the problem.

At this same school, Carter learned from the principal that boys thought themselves cool if they owned a semi-automatic weapon. The pregnancy rate was a problem, too, especially among sixth-graders. Carter thought the problem was serious enough that people should know about it, so he shared the story in speeches around the country. "That's not Bangladesh; that's not Haiti," Carter told audiences. "That's Atlanta. That's my next-door neighbor."[6]

As he has shown around the world, when a neighbor needs help, Jimmy Carter will be the first person knocking on the door.

Chapter Notes

Chapter 1. The Fight for Peace, 1978

1. Jimmy Carter, *Keeping Faith* (New York: Bantam Books, 1982), p. 391.

2. Ibid.

3. Jimmy Carter, *Talking Peace: A Vision for the Next Generation* (New York: Puffin Books), p. 17.

Chapter 2. Growing Up, 1924–1942

1. *A New Spirit, A New Commitment, A New America: The Official 1977 Inaugural Book* (New York: Bantam Books, 1977), p. 33.

2. Marie B. Allen, "Oral History Interview with Rachel Clark." (Dated November 9, 1978; stored in Jimmy Carter Library), p. 7.

3. Jimmy Carter interview on *The Today Show* (NBC Television), autumn 2000.

Chapter 3. Rising to the Presidency, 1943–1972

1. Jimmy Carter, *Why Not The Best?* (Nashville: Broadman Press, 1975), p. 62.

2. *A New Spirit, A New Commitment, A New America: The Official 1977 Inaugural Book* (New York: Bantam Books, 1977), p. 40.

3. Ibid., p. 43.

Chapter 4. Election to the White House, 1973–1976

1. Bonnie Angelo, *First Mothers* (New York: William Morrow, 2000), p. 283.

2. Kandy Stroud, *How Jimmy Won* (New York: William Morrow and Company, Inc., 1997), p. 394.

3. Gerald R. Ford, *A Time To Heal* (New York: Harper & Row, 1979), p. 441.

Chapter 5. Issues in Office, 1976–1980

1. Letter, Patricia Reno to President Carter, April 15, 1977. (Weekly Presidential Mail Sample, Box #1, Jimmy Carter Library).

2. Response, President Carter to Patricia Reno, April 22, 1977. (Weekly Presidential Mail Sample, Box #1, Jimmy Carter Library).

Chapter 6. After the Presidency

1. Jimmy Carter, *Talking Peace* (New York: Puffin Books, 1995), p. 122.

2. Ryan Cooley and Lily Smith, "Solving Those Conflicts!," *Buffalo News*, Fall 1999.

3. Author interview with Carrie Harmon, 2000.

4. Ibid.

5. Tim O'Shei, "City Welcomes Ex-president," *The Sun* (Hamburg, New York), March 25, 1993, pp. 1, 15.

6. Ibid.

Further Reading

Carter, Jimmy. *An Outdoor Journal: Adventures & Reflections.* New York: Bantam Books, 1988.

———. *Keeping Faith: Memoirs of a President.* New York: Bantam Books, 1983.

———. *Talking Peace with Jimmy Carter: The Close-Up Foundation.* New York: N A L, 1995.

George, Linda and Charles George. *Jimmy Carter: Builder of Peace.* Danbury, Conn.: Children's Press, 2000.

Joseph, Paul. *Jimmy Carter.* Edina, Minn.: ABDO Publishing Company, Inc., 1998.

Lindop, Edmund. *Richard M. Nixon, Jimmy Carter, Ronald Reagan.* Brookfield, Conn.: Twenty-First Century Books, Inc., 1996.

Lucas, Eileen. *Nixon, Ford, & Carter.* Rourke Corporation, Vero Beach, Fla., 1996.

Richman, Daniel A. *James E. Carter: 39th President of the United States.* Ada, Okla.: Garrett Educational Corporation, 1989.

Schraff, Anne. *Jimmy Carter.* Springfield, N.J.: Enslow Publishers, Inc., 1998.

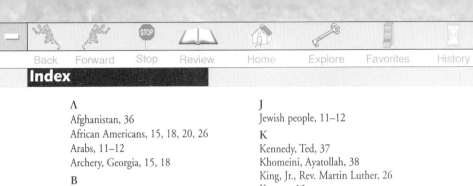

Index

A
Afghanistan, 36
African Americans, 15, 18, 20, 26
Arabs, 11–12
Archery, Georgia, 15, 18

B
Begin, Menachem, 11, 13–14, 34
Brezhnev, Leonid, 36

C
Camp David, 11–12, 13, 38
Carter, Amy, 26, 28, 30
Carter, Billy, 15
Carter, Chip, 23
Carter, Earl, 15, 20, 23
Carter, Gloria, 15
Carter, Jack, 22
Carter, Jeffrey, 23
Carter, Lillian, 15–16, 20, 23, 27
Carter, Rosalynn Smith, 21–22, 23, 26,
    30–31, 39, 41, 42–43
Carter, Ruth, 15, 21
Carter Center, 40, 42–43
Carter's Warehouse, 23–24
China, 35
civil rights, 19–20, 25
Clark, Jack, 20
Clark, Rachel, 20
Coleman, Julia, 17–18

D
Davis, A. D., 18, 19–20
Democratic National Headquarters, 27

E
Egypt, 11, 13–14, 37, 41
Eritrea, 39
Ethiopia, 39

F
Ford, Gerald, 27–28, 29, 32, 34, 41–42

G
Gaza Strip, 12
Georgia Planning Committee, 24
Golan Heights, 12
Great Britain, 11

H
Habitat for Humanity, 43–44

I
Israel, 11, 13–14

J
Jewish people, 11–12

K
Kennedy, Ted, 37
Khomeini, Ayatollah, 38
King, Jr., Rev. Martin Luther, 26
Knesset, 13

L
League of Nations, 11

M
Mississippi, 22
Mondale, Walter, 28
Moscow, 35–36

N
National Energy Act, 34
Nixon, Richard, 27–28

O
Organization of Petroleum Exporting
    Countries (OPEC), 33

P
Pahlavi, Reza Shah, 37–38
Palestine, 11–12
Panama Canal, 35
Pentagon, 39
Plains, Georgia, 15, 17–18, 21, 24, 40, 42

R
Reagan, Ronald, 37–38

S
Sadat, Anwar, 11, 13–14, 34, 41
Sinai Peninsula, 12

T
Teheran, Iran, 37
The Atlanta Project, 42
"30 Questions Test," 25
Three Mile Island, 34

U
United States Navy, 21, 23

V
Vance, Cyrus, 11, 13

W
Watergate, 27
West Bank, 12
White Citizens Council, 24
World Trade Center, 39
WWI, 11